Last of the Human Freedoms

Choosing the Road to Redemption

Victor Aguirre

Copyright © 2019 Victor Aguirre

All rights reserved.

ISBN: **9781070162256**

Victor Aguirre

DEDICATION

First and foremost, I would like to dedicate this book to my beautiful wife Beatriz Flores. Bety, it is true, a man's success depends on the kind of woman he chooses to have in his life. My success would not be possible without you.

I also have to send a big shout out to my daughter Sylvia Cera who has been through a tougher road than mine – and flourished. Sylvia, thank you for being the cause behind my redemption. I love you and RJ.

Lots of love to my brothers and sisters: Alex, Claudia, Rene, Christy, Eddie, but especially Mireya Neria who has been my biggest supporter since day one.

To my mother, "Ama, la quiero mucho y agradezco todos los sacrificios que hiso para sacarnos adelante."

I also want to thank Greg and Deanna Steele who have been a big part of my journey since I was released from prison. Because of their love and support, my wife and I have been able to do more for others. They have been a couple we admire and look up to. Love you guys.

CHAPTER 1

Beginnings

"If there is anything that we wish to change in the child, we should first examine it

and see whether it is not something that could be better changed in ourselves."

- C.G. Jung, Integration of the Personality

He lay on his back staring at the ceiling. He could not believe the situation he was now in. He was only 16 years old! "How could this have happened to me! Why me!" he kept repeating to himself over and over again.

The guard passed by his cell to count and check on him. He looked in and walked away aloofly as if no one was there. He didn't ask any questions and didn't appear to care that this little kid was in a cage. This made the young boy feel more alone. The loneliness and solitude were eating at his spirit. He did not believe that he would have to stay in this cage for long. It felt subhuman to him. "I will die of loneliness if I have to stay here much longer. I need to be around people, to feel the sun on my skin, to move around freely," he said to himself. For sure someone would come and rescue him soon. He wanted to scream and beg for help.

His cell was small. The bathroom at his house was bigger. There was a concrete slab attached to the wall with a thin, plastic mattress on it. A smaller slab next to that served as a desk. A metal stool was fixed to the floor and the stainless-steel toilet was next to the door. A thin and horizontal window adorned the top of one of the walls. That's it. All this in a space the size of a regular house closet.

He spent most of his time looking out the window. He would roll his mattress up and stand on it so he could see the outside. The detention center was behind the very popular Ascarate Lake and he could see lines of traffic passing on the street on their way to go fishing or to the family picnic. He longingly stared at the random people walking by – carrying groceries, listening to their Walkman, jogging. He even saw kids going to and from school. Kids his age. Kids who didn't know that someone just like them was in a cell all alone only yards away. He was surprised that life outside kept rolling along as if nothing had happened. In his mind, the whole world should have stopped and mourned with him. But it had not.

Most of the time the scene outside became blurry from the tears of sadness bubbling in his eyes. "How did I get myself into this mess," his soul would whisper to no one in particular.

Victor was born in Cd. Juarez, Chihuahua, Mexico. His mother Guadalupe was 15 years old when he was born. He was named after his father even though his father did not play a big part in raising him.

Juarez was a suffocating place. Juarez is a Mexican city which lies on the Rio Grande (Rio Bravo to Mexicans), south of El Paso, Texas. A majority of the city's population lives in poverty. Juarez is infamously known as the place where women's bodies turn up dead in the middle of the desert and no one knows who killed and dumped them there. Over 370 young women, Las Muertas de Juarez as they are known, have been killed and dumped over the years without a trace of their killer or killers. Some say this is the work of a seriously deranged serial killer. Others whisper the women were kidnapped, used as sex slaves for the military and killed when they were no longer wanted or needed. And the final, solve-all explanation, is that the murders were cartel related.

At one point, Juarez was known as the most dangerous city in the world, reaching close to 200 murders MONTHLY – even more dangerous and deadly than countries at war. Juarez has always been a rough city.

The neighborhood Victor and his mom lived in was the poorest one in Juarez and one of the poorest in all of Mexico. It was a gray place, literally. Lifeless. The desert gave it a very barren and dead feel. It was not a green place. Plant life and trees did not thrive there. The dry desert had a big part to do with that, although one could argue that Juarez was so dangerous to life that even trees and plants refused to grow there in protest. In this neighborhood dust clung to everything, making it look filthy. Even the people seemed to be continuously covered in dirt. It did not matter if you showered or bathed, dirt would soon find you and hug you for dear life.

There were no paved streets and dust was always floating in the air like clouds. Trash littered every empty space. Undernourished dogs, ribs showing, walked around with flies buzzing over them scavenging for whatever meal they could find.

Their mournful facial expressions were human-like. If they could verbalize their emotions, they would say, "What did I do to deserve this!?"

It did not take long for Guadalupe to become tired and weary of this place. It was not fit for human life. She made a promise to herself that one day she would flee and never come back. From the house they lived in they could actually see "el otro lado", the other side. El Paso, Texas was literally a stone-throw away from Juarez. The contrast between the two countries was shocking. Looking across the river from atop the hill, Guadalupe and Victor could see beautifully paved roads and well-manicured lawns. The University of Texas at El Paso (UTEP), with its oriental architecture, was a shining jewel of a building nestled in the mountains of El Paso. To their right was the Civic Center, which looked like a giant bowl, and all of the buildings in the downtown area. Looking across was always a stark reminder to Guadalupe that she needed to cross the river and head to El Paso for a better life as soon as possible.

If you were in El Paso looking across the river, the sight was totally different. From that vantage point, you would see a cluster of worn-down houses and shanties sitting atop rugged, rocky hills and beaten, rusted cars or buses sending plumes of toxic smoke in the air traveling on unpaved roads. It was almost impossible to believe that two countries, so close together, could be so far apart economically, socially and politically.

Guadalupe made the decision to leave Juarez shortly after she turned 18. By this time, she had given birth to a little baby girl, Victor's little sister, Mireya. The only option she had was to cross the the river illegally. She had dropped out of school out of necessity after 6th grade and did not know how to apply for a visa to the U.S or to follow any of those processes. She felt her only option was to cross illegally. All she wanted was a better life for herself and her two children and nothing was going to get in her way of that – most definitely not a river.

Crossing over the river had never been too difficult. People walked across all the time, using the backroads and the hidden places, of course. If the river was full, as happened after heavy rain, people would have to be craftier to wade across.

Crossing would not be hard for her. She had done it many times before just for fun. The hard part was having to leave her two children behind with her mother. She could not take them with her into the unknown. Would she find a job? Would she find a place to live? Would she blend in and understand the culture?

Would that culture understand hers? These were questions and problems she needed to face alone for their own good.

She promised she would return for them as soon as she had found a job and a place to live. She did not know when exactly this would be. It could be a few months or a few years. But she knew she would return for them one day. Victor and Mireya were too young to understand they were being left behind and would not see their mother for a long time. They were sad to see their mother leave, but their grandmother, lovingly nicknamed "Chachita", was a beautiful soul and was the perfect person to keep them safe and happy while Guadalupe was gone.

Chachita, in typical Mexican grandma fashion, was the kind of woman who cared about others more than she cared about herself, especially when her grandkids were involved. Her small house was always full of kids – cousins, siblings, you name it. She was the de-facto mother to all of them. They never felt poor because of her. She made sure there was always food on the table and her meals felt like feasts – even when it was just beans and tortillas.

Her house was host to all holidays and birthdays. Anytime something needed to be celebrated, it was celebrated at Chachitas'. Mexicans are known for their love of fiestas and celebrations and the entire family loved getting together at Chachitas' for any and all celebrations. Victor and Mireya were lucky to have a grandma like her.

CHAPTER 2

Running for the Border

"Give me your tired, your poor, your huddled masses

Yearning to breathe free. The wretched refuse of your teeming shore.

Send these, the homeless, tempest-tossed, to me: I lift

my lamp beside the golden door."

- Emma Lazarus

The day Guadalupe returned for Victor and Mireya was one of the happiest days of her life. She had finally found a job as a waitress and had found a beaten down trailer for them to live in. The trailer wasn't much better, nor bigger, than Chachita's humble home, but it was in the United States and to her this felt like opportunity – the land where dreams come true. Victor was about to be five years old and Mireya was about to turn three. Guadalupe was eager to get her two children and cross them over. She felt hopeful and optimistic and was proud that she had finally fulfilled the promise she had made to herself and them years ago. She just knew things were going to be a lot better than in this God-forgotten part of the world.

After saying their teary good-byes to their cousins and to Chachita, they headed towards the river which flowed a few blocks from Chachita's home. Having to leave their loved ones was painful. As poor as this place was, it was still the only place they knew. The only place they could call home. It was excruciating having to leave everyone and everything behind in search of a better life. You lose a part of your being, a part of your soul, when you are forced to flee the place you have loved as your own.

Victor did not understand what a "coyote" was. He thought it was a wolf. During their march to the river, Guadalupe was explaining to Victor and Mireya that they needed to stay as quiet as possible, to not make any noise, and to listen to all the instructions which would be given by "el coyote." In their young mind, Victor and Mireya thought there would be a magical wolf waiting to guide them with his staff into the promised land.

Usually, Guadalupe would cross back and forth between Mexico and the U.S. by herself. You could literally walk over some parts of the Rio Grande and crossing over was as easy as a walk to the neighborhood store. You just had to know where and when. This crossing would be a little more difficult because she had two small children in tow and Guadalupe did not want to risk being caught. The stakes were too high and she decided to pay a "coyote," an expert in illegal crossings, for the trip north.

It was getting dark and this was the perfect moment to cross without being detected and caught by the Border Patrol. Other families who were also making the trip across the river had gathered around the coyote to hear the instructions he was giving. After agreeing to everything he had said, everyone handed him their money and the trek towards the land of milk and honey began.

The coyote walked in front of them confidently. This was his territory, his domain. He knew where the risky areas where and steered clear of them. He was peeking over bushes, signaling for them to hustle behind him quietly, whispering instructions along the way. "Paren!" (stop!), "Tirense al piso" (get on the floor!), "No se muevan!" (don't move!). A few times they actually saw the Border Patrol pass by as they were hiding. They all followed instructions perfectly. Victor and Mireya did not say a word. The fear of being caught was stronger than the need to talk.

After a few hours of waiting, walking, ducking and crawling, they made it to *El Paso* safely. They all thanked the coyote and walked away, each family towards their own destination and destiny. A few people had family and friends waiting for them in cars to take them away.

They were now in the land of the free. A land which promised an American dream.

Life in El Paso was not much better for Victor and Mireya. They were still living in extreme poverty. Guadalupe was a very young mother. Living in a foreign land, alone, was very difficult for her. She was a teenager. Emotionally, she was a wreck. She missed her family. Mexicans, no matter how poor, value family over everything. Guadalupe was no exception. Two thoughts conflicted in her mind and tore her spirit apart: wanting to be with her family in Juarez and fighting for a better life for her kids and for herself. Why couldn't she have both of them at the same time? Why did it have to be one or the other? There were no opportunities for her in Juarez. She knew this. And yet she missed that place because that's where her loved ones were.

Not long after bringing her kids to El Paso, she began using drugs. The drugs eased her pain and misery. The money she was making as a waitress was not enough to feed two hungry kids, pay the bills and a drug habit. She began selling her body to pay for the drugs and to make other ends meet. There were days when Victor and Mireya would wake up and see a different man leaving their mother's bedroom. Guadalupe hated what she was becoming, but she felt trapped and didn't see a way out. When times were specifically difficult, Guadalupe would go sell her blood at a plasma center – "la plasma." They would often see Guadalupe walking towards their trailer carrying groceries with a cotton swab taped to her arm where the plasma needle had been inserted.

The worst mistake Guadalupe made in El Paso was falling in love with Miguel. Life with him in the picture was a disaster. Their courtship was fast and furious - a toxic mix which was clearly going to explode and take everyone down as collateral. She was young and used drugs. He was a lot older than her. But he was a U.S. citizen and Guadalupe saw the relationship as an advantage for her and her kids. Maybe through him they could all become legal citizens here in America.

Miguel was a total bully. He would physically abuse Guadalupe for the smallest of things. He was an alcoholic and when he was drunk everyone was terrified. Guadalupe received the worst beatings from him when he had alcohol in his blood. Victor and Mireya were not immune to the beatings. Miguel would grab any item within reach and beat them mercilessly for the smallest of reasons. Sometimes for no reason at all. Their trailer was always full of screams and violence and cop cars.

Guadalupe gave birth to two children from Miguel. Alex and Claudia were born one year apart. Not long after their birth, Miguel began sexually abusing Mireya. Victor felt helpless. He knew what was happening to his younger sister but was too young to intervene. He wanted to kill Miguel. He fantasized about doing something horrible to him. Mutilate him. Cut him up in a million pieces slowly and watch him scream out in pain until his last breath. He wanted to inflict the same pain on Miguel that Miguel was inflicting on everyone else. These feelings were very conflicting for Victor because he was a peaceful kid. He didn't like violence. On the contrary, he hated it.

Victor felt like a coward. How could you let your sister be violated and not do something about it? How could you watch your mother get beaten half to death, turned into a bloody pulp before your very eyes and just stand there and cry. It didn't matter that Victor was only 9 years old. Victor felt like he was a coward for doing nothing.

CHAPTER 3

Separation

"A kind gesture can reach a wound that only compassion can heal."

- Steve Maraboli

The beatings and the sexual abuse had gotten too obvious for everyone to ignore. Teachers were beginning to ask why there were bruises on Victor's and Mireya's bodies. Neighbors had begun whispering amongst each other that horrible things were happening to the kids next door. They could hear the screams of agony and pain. They saw their sad faces, always looking at the floor and terrified of everything. They smelled of urine and filth. Their clothes were always torn and tattered. They definitely needed a shower.

One of the neighbors decided to act. She called the Child Protective Services to report the physical abuse and suspicion of sexual abuse and requested an investigation into the living conditions of the kids next door.An investigator went to the house and found things worse than what had been reported.

"The Texas Department of Human Services became involved with Guadalupe Cardenas and her family in October, involving reports of physical abuse, neglectful supervision and sexual abuse. The kids were found alone and the home was found under unsanitary conditions by police. The home was infested by cockroaches, the children were extremely dirty and had not been fed. A strong smell of urine could be detected throughout the house. The children were extremely dirty and very much in need of a bath. The two smallest children were infested with lice," her report stated.

After finding out what was happening to the kids, they took them all away to foster care. The four siblings were separated. Victor went to one foster family and his siblings to others. By this time Victor was angry at the world. The shy, respectful kid started boiling from within. His anger consumed him. He was angry at Miguel. He was angry at himself for letting things happen to his mom and sister. But he was especially angry at his mother for everything that was happening. He blamed her for bringing Miguel into their life and turning it into a living hell. Before, they had just been poor. Now, their life had become a nightmare.

There were times when Victor's angered overpowered him so much that he would fling his mattress all over the room in a fit of rage. He would yell and scream and punch the walls or the doors like a wounded animal. He looked, and felt, possessed. He did not know how to deal with all these crazy emotions bubbling inside his heart.

Guadalupe was allowed to visit the kids at the offices of Child Protective Services once a week. The CPS officers provided a room and let her spend up to two hours alone with all four of her kids. Victor refused to visit with her. No matter how much begging and pleading he received from his foster family and case worker, he refused to go see her. Guadalupe was crushed. And so was Victor.

During the next few years Victor and his siblings were in and out of foster homes. Sometimes they would be back with Guadalupe in a few weeks, sometimes in a few months. After being returned to their home things would run smoothly for a while, until Guadalupe got the urge to use again or to neglect the kids and then back to foster care they went.

CHAPTER 4

The Neighborhood Gang

"When I look at it carefully, by examining the interviews and the various social scientists'

studies, it becomes easy for me to see we are all just rebelling......We were rebelling

and crying out for our fathers. We were rebelling against the home conditions that

existed in our communities. We needed our fathers, but above all we wanted to be loved and

accepted by them. Since we couldn't find it at home and in our respective communities, we created it for ourselves."

-Drexel Deal, The Fight of My Life is Wrapped Up in My Father

After the authorities forced Miguel out of the picture, there was a period of semi-peace. Campestre was a forgotten neighborhood on the outskirts of El Paso in the small town of Socorro. It reminded Victor of his childhood in Juarez. Most of the roads were not paved. Some houses were made out of pallets and cardboard and tin metal and whatever else people could find to protect themselves from the elements. Most homes did not have proper sewage systems. The neighborhood smelled like shit – literally. And yet, it still felt better than all the places Victor and family had lived before. Cotton and corn fields surrounded the place, giving it a small country town feel. You could almost imagine the men riding horses and chopping wood while the women were outside hanging clothes to dry and the children milked the cows. To the south, the Rio Grande snaked from East to West a few blocks from their new home.

Guadalupe had moved the family here to get away from the past. She wanted a fresh start and she desperately wanted to get away from the prying eyes of her other neighbors. The shame of what they had gone through was too much to bear. Guadalupe was ashamed and wanted to get away to a place where no one knew who they were. But, Campestre was not the place it appeared or felt to be. It had a dark side and Victor would soon get caught up in its underbelly.

Victor was 12 years old when he joined the neighborhood gang. The Barrio Campestre Locos (BCL) gang was made up of close to 100 kids, mostly teenagers. Most of them were from similar backgrounds as Victor. All were dirt poor. Most came from broken homes, had a chip on their shoulder, and wanted to prove their worth to the world.

Victor did not ask to join the gang. He was assimilated into it. At school he would hang around the kids from his neighborhood, most of who were members of BCL. One day in middle school, Victor was sitting on the bleachers with his girlfriend and saw a group of gang members who were not part of the school walking towards some of his friends from Campestre. From experience, he knew that these kids were looking for trouble. Gang fights were a common occurrence at this middle school. Some of the kids were holding bats and sticks and some were wearing "brass knuckles" on their hands. They were definitely looking for a fight.

Victor left his girlfriend and ran over to his friends who were on the basketball court waiting for the intruders. The kids from Campestre were heavily outnumbered. No matter how tough they pretended to be, they were scared. Victor was scared as well. But he could not let his friends fight alone. At that age he was more scared of not being accepted, of being ridiculed and branded as weak by his friends than he was of a beating. So, he stood with his friends.

   The beating the kids from Campestre received was severe. The Barrio Nuevo (BN) gang members let them have it without mercy. Even some of the female "cholas" from Campestre were beaten mercilessly. If someone fell to the ground, a mob would descend on him or her and attack viciously, like hyenas hunting its prey. The "crack" of wood making contact with flesh and bones was deafening. Blood gushed from almost every kid from Campestre. The brutality of it all was a reflection of the pain and anger those kids were holding inside. It was as if they were taking revenge on every single person who had hurt them in the past. Victor would have done the same thing to them if he had the chance. He was sure it was Miguel's face he would be beating every time he swung the bat or kicked someone on the floor.

   After hearing all the commotion, teachers and other adults ran to the basketball courts to stop the fighting. The BN kids began their retreat laughing and jeering and threatening everyone who was not one of them.

   Some of the BN kids were students at the school and they were all immediately suspended. Victor was shocked when they called him into the office to tell him that he would be suspended as well for "participating in a riot." He didn't' think he had participated in anything but getting a brutal ass kicking. But every kid on the basketball court, victim and attacker, was suspended from school because of the school's zero tolerance policy concerning gangs. The fact that the school had a zero-tolerance policy on gang activity was evidence enough that this community, and Victor himself, was facing a rude awakening.

Victor was scared of the suspension. Guadalupe was going to be furious when she found out he had been suspended and he knew she was going to beat him for it. His arm had been put on a shoulder sling at the school infirmary, and he had a busted lip, along with other bumps and bruises from being hit with limbs and objects. His shirt was sticky with dried blood. Now he had to wait and see what kind of beating he was going to get at home.

He did not have to wait long to find out what Guadalupe had in store for him. She slapped him as soon as he walked in the door and furiously demanded to know what had caused him to get suspended. Every time he tried to explain she called him a liar and slapped him harder until she worked herself into a frenzy. Maybe she was taking revenge on Miguel, too?

After this school incident, a tighter bond developed between Victor and his friends from Campestre. They felt like brothers now. In the neighborhood, all the other teenagers were talking about the school fight as if it was a mythological event. Everyone who had fought against the BN members was lauded as a hero. The older teenagers who were either in high school or had dropped out of school, congratulated and honored the "warriors" who fought valiantly against BN. The neighborhood cholas flocked to them as if they were heroes of war. Victor felt a pride he hadn't felt in a long time. He felt he belonged and was accepted. He felt useful and wanted. He felt part of a family. It was then that he knew exactly what he was missing from his life. And now that he had found it, he was not letting it go.

To be an official member of the Barrio Campestre Locos you had to go through what's called an "initiation." An initiation was simple: you had to fight four or five members of BCL at the same time for a few minutes. If you fought hard, if you did not quit or show weakness, then you would become a full-fledged member of the gang. If you did show weakness or quit, they would beat you up again and tell you to leave and never come around again. The whole group who beat you and witnessed the beating would grade your courage after the initiation and vote on whether you deserved membership.

Victor had thought about getting "initiated" before, but never followed through with it. An ass-whooping was an ass-whooping and Victor didn't feel like going through all of that. But ever since the school fight his friends, members of BCL, had been asking him to join, to get initiated. Victor always told them he was thinking about it.

A few weeks after the school incident, Victor and a couple of BCL members were sitting around smoking marijuana under a tree by the neighborhood canal. The subject of Victor's initiation was not mentioned at all. Suddenly, Manny, also known as Spanky, jumped up and sucker-punched Victor in the face. The other two teens who were there also jumped in and began attacking him. Victor was trying hard to fend off the punches but had been caught totally off guard. They kicked and stomped and punched him for what seemed like an eternity. Victor didn't know what was going on. He thought maybe he had done something wrong and was being beaten for it. That's what gangs do if someone violates a rule or the gang's code of conduct – they beat you for it. How bad depends on how bad the infraction is.

And then it stopped. Victor lay on the ground bleeding and trying to catch his breath. His left ear was ringing from a kick to it. Manny held out his hand and helped Victor off the ground. "Ahora si ya eres de Campestre, homeboy." Everyone there took a turn giving Victor a handshake, hug and welcomed him as a full member of the gang. Victor felt on top of the world despite the aches and pains on his body.

That is how Victor became a member of the BCL gang.

CHAPTER 5

Chickens Coming Home to Roost

"Nobody ever did, or ever will, escape the consequences of his choices."

-Alfred A. Montapert

In three years of gang membership, Victor had completely ruined his life. Like most of his homies, he began to use drugs and using drugs is always the beginning of ruin. He started smoking marijuana exclusively. Marijuana was his favorite drug. When he smoked it, he felt like the world was a peaceful place. All the pain of his existence, the self-hate and shame, blew away every time he exhaled the smoke.

The first time he smoked it he could not stop laughing. He laughed and laughed and laughed some more. His friends began to worry that he had lost his mind. One of the older teenagers who was there was scared that Victor had gone crazy. He was only twelve years old and the older teenager knew that he could get in big trouble if something happened to this stupid kid who he had given marijuana to and was now laughing out of his brain in his house. He told the other kids to give Victor some water or to wet a towel and put it over his head. This only made Victor laugh harder. He just couldn't stop. Slowly but surely the laughing stopped. But the smile on Victor's face was still there. He was hooked. Life was perfect under the effects of THC.

The experience with marijuana led Victor to experiment with other drugs in search of that blissful, peaceful feeling. He wanted to continue altering his consciousness and jumping into a different reality than the one he lived in. He tried cocaine, pills, smoked heroin and, worst of all, started huffing spray paint. Anything was better than sobriety and the pain in his soul.

At school his grades dropped. He lived in the principal's office. Fighting, talking back to the teachers, bringing weapons to school were all incidents he was suspended for. Due to all the disciplinary problems, he was sent to Alternative school numerous times. Alternative school had a more rigid environment, almost like a prison, and the powers that be felt this was the only place other kids and teachers at regular school would be safe from his behavior.

Throughout his childhood, Victor had been a very good baseball player. He loved all sports. He loved competition and athletics. In middle school he played football and ran track and boxed. But baseball was his passion. He felt alive on the baseball field. At home he had accumulated trophies and medals for his excellence in baseball. He had other trophies as well, but none meant more to him than the baseball trophies. Some of his coaches told him he would be a baseball star one day. He believed them and hoped it was true.

The gang and the drug use ruined all those dreams. He was a wreck. In 9th grade he impregnated his girlfriend. He was 15 years old. She was 17. He definitely was not ready to be a father. He was a child himself. How could he take care of another person if he didn't know how to take care of himself? The problem was that the pregnancy, like so many teenage pregnancies, was not planned. He had unprotected sex with his girlfriend, she became pregnant, and that was that. Even if it had been planned, Victor was a little kid and would not be able to raise a child the right way.

Victor did not see his girlfriend's pregnancy as a life-changing event. He was too immature to give it any importance. In his neighborhood, teenagers like him became mothers and fathers on a consistent basis and nothing changed. It was just part of the environment, another day at the office, as they say. He continued doing what he was doing, oblivious to the fact that a small child would soon need his guidance and protection.

His school counselors and coaches tried to help him get off the drugs and get out of the gang. They saw potential in him. He really wasn't a bad kid. They saw something worth saving. They knew he needed to get on the right track now that his girlfriend was pregnant. They tried enrolling him in different programs, they tried mentoring and counseling him. Nothing worked. Victor was damaged goods.

After another disciplinary incident at the Alternative school he was in, he was placed in a drug rehab center for juveniles. A few weeks into the program, he snuck out in the wee hours of the night because he missed being around his friends and the drugs and the gang fights. Leaving the drug rehab center was a very costly mistake.

The day that changed everything was strange. The streets felt quieter than usual. Even the trees around the neighborhood seemed to be holding still as if they knew something horrible was going to happen.

  A few days earlier, Victor had run away from the drug rehab center he had been placed in. He was now sitting in front of his house smoking a joint when his friend Spanky, the one who had begun Victor's initiation into the gang with a sucker punch, stopped by in his car. Spanky was 18 years old. He was somewhat of a loose cannon. Other gang members, from Campestre and other gangs, feared crossing him. He would not hesitate to pull a knife or gun on you if he felt you disrespected him in some way. He didn't care if people were around to see or not. Like Victor, he was also an expectant father. Teenage pregnancies were common in Campestre.

  Spanky was trying to get his life together. He had graduated from high school and now that his girlfriend was with child, he had begun working for some sort of construction company. The company offered him a great opportunity and, in a few days, he would be moving his family to another state to get away from the gangs and the drugs and the temptations of the El Paso streets. But he wanted to leave with a bang. He wanted to party one last time as if it was his last day on earth.

  When he saw Victor in front of his house he stopped and got out of his car. He took the joint Victor offered him and inhaled as much smoke as would fit in his lungs. He told Victor that he was leaving in a few days and that he had arranged a party with two hot female friends of his. He needed Victor to come with him tonight and "help" him with one of the girls while he "did his thing" with the other one. Victor laughed and accepted the offer. They talked and planned and agreed to meet later on that night. They agreed that Spanky would go to his house to take a shower and clean up and then would return for Victor in an hour or two so they could go pick up the girls and go to a hotel. Victor asked Spanky to give him a ride to Little Cricket's house. Spanky could pick him up from there later on that evening.

At Cricket's house Victor continued smoking marijuana with the few other gang members there. When Spanky arrived for Victor a few hours later, the plan to go out with the two girls was ditched. Everyone decided to go buy more drugs and alcohol and party in the car. They drove around drinking and smoking and snorting cocaine. At some point during the night someone put out the idea that they should go get a gun and go look for the "B-Enners" (members of the rival BN gang, or Barrio Nuevo). "Simon," everyone said in one voice.

They headed towards Victor's house. Victor had recently bought a 12-gauge shotgun and a 22. long-range rifle from another BCL gang member. When they arrived at his house, Victor got off and went for the rifle. It had 19 shots and he thought it would do more damage if they were caught in a gun fight with BN members. When he jumped in the car, he checked to make sure the rifle was fully loaded and ready to fire if needed. He put the rifle between the front seats and they headed for BN.

When they reached the rival neighborhood, Spanky slowed the car to a crawl and turned off the headlights. They wanted to catch them by surprise. Victor was itching to see someone he could shoot at. He wanted to show his homies how bad, tough and heartless he was. He still held a grudge against BN for the beating they gave him when he was in middle school.

They saw no one. They looked in every street, around every corner where the BN members were known to hang out. They saw no one. It was getting close to midnight, but it was Friday night and Friday nights were party nights for all gang members. It was shocking not to find at least one BN member they could shoot at.

After looking around and finding no one, "Shorty" told everyone that there was a party in Moon City. Moon City was another rival neighborhood and it was only a few blocks away from BN. To anyone coming from the outside, all these neighborhoods –

Campestre, Barrio Nuevo, Moon City - would look the same. They all had the same social and economic conditions. They were all poor communities trying to survive any way they could. Nothing really separated one from the other. They were so close together they could have been one big neighborhood and no one would have noticed the difference. However, the gangs had drawn imaginary lines and divided the area into the warzone it had become.

Victor's girlfriend and three-month-old daughter lived in Moon City and her cousins were all members of MCL (Moon City Locos). The party Shorty was talking about was actually a birthday party for "Piojo," who was a cousin of Victor's girlfriend and the party was being held at her house. Victor told them that he knew exactly where the party was because his girlfriend was hosting it.

He hatched a plan. Victor told them that he would get off the car first, go to the party with the gun hidden under his jacket, demand to see his girlfriend and daughter and if they refused to let him in or attacked him he would shoot them. It was a pea-brain plan, but to Victor's intoxicated juvenile mind it seemed like the perfect macho thing to do.

On their way to Moon City, Spanky kept passing out behind the wheel. He was so drunk and high from the mixture of drugs they were taking that he could no longer pay attention to the steering wheel. Victor made him stop the car and traded places with him so he could drive.

It was past midnight and the streets seemed deserted and ghostly. He turned the corner from his girlfriend's house and could see the party from there. There were gang members on the street with liquor cups and bottles in their hands and the music blaring through the neighborhood. Victor inched forward at a crawl. He could not feel the adrenaline because of the drug haze in his mind. He could not feel fear or worry or any emotion. It was as if he had become a zombie. The drugs had numbed him perfectly. Or horribly.

As he inched closer and got close enough to the party, some members of MCL saw him and Spanky in the front seat and went into a frenzy. They started throwing the MCL gang sign with their twisted fingers and began yelling obscenities and rushing towards the car. A beer bottle just missed the windshield.

Spanky picked up the rifle quickly, hung out of the passenger side window and started firing at the crowd. The shots were like loud thunderclaps.

Bang! Bang! Bang!! Bangbangbangbang!!

Everyone was running for cover, jumping to the ground or behind cars. The flashes of the gun were blinding and lighted the black of the night. The inside of the car seemed to be on fire. Victor saw someone jerk forward and collapse on the ground. Time slowed to a crawl. Everything was happening in slow motion, as if someone had pressed a button on a remote and frozen the time-space continuum.

After what seemed like an eternity, the gunshots stopped. Spanky slid back into his seat and time seemed to go back to normal just as quickly as it had changed to slow motion.

Victor drove out of the neighborhood in a frantic rush. The screeching tires were just as loud as the gunshots. Dust kicked up in the air. He was driving as fast as he could. His foot was pressed completely against the gas pedal. The loud bangs had awakened Victor's reasoning and now he knew he must fly out of the neighborhood without getting caught by the police or getting intercepted by the MCL's. It was a sure thing they had guns too. If they intercepted them, they would be able to shoot at them from the darkness and everyone in the car would be a sitting duck.

As they were heading to the main avenue, a police car saw them speeding and immediately turned on its headlights to give chase. Moon City was the worst place to have committed a drive-by shooting. The police station was only a few blocks from where the shooting had occurred and it was a certainty there would be cop cars in the vicinity.

Everyone in the car was screaming for Victor to drive faster. He tried to lose the cop car but couldn't. Within minutes, the entire police department seemed to be chasing after them. Victor tried to evade them to no avail. Everywhere he turned he saw the sirens flashing. There was no way they were going to get away from this one.

Victor saw a street coming up to his right and tried to make a sudden turn to surprise the pursuers. His foot was heavy on the gas pedal and the speed of the car turned that decision into a mistake for him. The momentum caused the car to swerve and fish-tail and almost flip over. He heard the frightened screams of everyone in the car. Somehow, he managed to gain control once again and continued down the street. He did not see the train tracks ahead of him and that was his final mistake. The tracks made the car jump in the air and land with a heavy thud on the pavement. Sparks came out from under the car and the impact shut down the engine. Spanky tossed the rifle out the window in a laughable attempt to get rid of it. The car then rolled to a stop.

All of the police officers got out of their vehicles and pointed their weapons at the car screaming, "Let us see your fucking hands!". One cop had a K-9 on a leash just in case they decided to run. Victor and his friends were screwed and they knew it. They were ordered to stick their hands out of the car and Victor was ordered to drop the car keys outside the vehicle.

One by one they came out of the car and were made to lay on the ground with their hands behind their head. When all of them were on the floor the police officers rushed in to put handcuffs on all five of them and place them in the backseat of their squad cars.

They were placed under arrest.

CHAPTER 6

Hanging in the Balance

"I am hanging in the balance of a perfect finished plan,
Like every sparrow falling, like every grain of sand."

-Bob Dylan

And now here he was, laying on his back staring at the ceiling. How in the world did he end up here? Was he dreaming? Did the events really happen? Did they really do a "drive-by" shooting at his girlfriend's house!? While his own three-month-old child was there? What if one of the shots had hit her? What if they had killed his own child? The thought alone gave him the creeps.

Nevertheless, here he was. In an extremely small cell. Only 16 years old and facing a murder charge. While in the police car, he heard a call over the police radio that a coroner was needed at the scene of the shooting, but he was too high to understand what was being said and what a coroner meant. Or maybe he just didn't want to face the reality he was in.

Here, in the loneliness and darkness of his cell he finally understood. One of the bullets had hit a teenager in the neck. The bullet hit the back of his neck and exited through his throat. Within minutes he was dead. Chocked on his own blood in front of his family, in front of other children. Paramedics could do nothing for him but watch him die. He was only 15 years old.

Victor knew this kid well. He knew him well because he was his girlfriend's little brother. Rigo was an uncle to Victor's daughter. He could not believe that this was happening. "Why!? Why!?," he would yell into his pillow with tears streaming down his face.

The tears were not only for him. Of course, he was scared of the future he was facing behind bars, but his tears were also for Rigo who was now dead at 15 years old, in the blooming stage of life. One of the 38 gang related murders committed that year in El Paso. The tears were for his daughter who would grow up without a father and an uncle; for his family, especially his sister Mireya whom he loved and wanted to protect always; and for his mother and his younger siblings, too. Victor knew in his heart that he was not a bad kid. He was not naturally violent. He had always been compassionate with others.

He remembered the first time his mother saw him dressed like a "cholo" gang banger. He was wearing a bandana around his head that almost covered his eyes. His flannel shirt was buttoned only with the top button and his pants were purposely too big for him, falling off his waist. "Why are you dressed like that!? You look ridiculous! That is not you. Why are you trying to be something you're not?", she had told him with sadness and anger in her voice. And as always, his mother had hit the nail in the head with that observation. She knew him better than he knew himself. She had carried him in her belly for nine months and had suckled him on her breasts. She knew this was not her son.

Deep down, maybe subconsciously, *he* knew she was right. This life he had chosen was not his own. It just wasn't him.

After three months in the juvenile detention center, Victor was transferred to the county jail to face the murder charges against him as an adult. Texas law permitted juveniles to be tried in adult courts if the crime committed was serious. Murder was as serious as it could get. Victor had been charged with murder even though he was not the one who fired the shots which killed Rigo. Texas had an infamous law called the "law of parties." This law allowed the state to charge people with a crime committed if they knew the crime was going to be committed and/or were present when it was committed. Basically, the principle is that to be guilty of a crime, you don't need to have actually committed it. You need only to have helped the thing take place. Even just knowing it was about to happen and not trying to stop it is enough.

Robberies are a good example to use in explaining this law. Let's assume two people went to rob a store. One goes in the store to do the robbery while the other one stays outside to be the lookout. During the robbery, the one inside the store decides to kill everyone there. Under the "law of parties," the person outside the store will be charged with every murder inside the store even though he never pulled the trigger. That's how the law of parties worked. So, technically, Victor had not murdered anyone, but because he knew there was a gun in the car (his gun) and knew the shots would be fired he was charged with murder.

In the county jail, he was placed in a cellblock with other juveniles who, like him, had been transferred to the adult system due to the seriousness of their crimes. There were other teens there who were facing murder charges themselves. Some were being charged with armed robberies, others with car-jackings. Victor saw a lot of faces he knew from his stay in the juvenile detention center. Every serious crime on the books seemed to be represented here. Most of the kids were gang members from around town.

It was a jungle.

The only authority the kids respected was their own. Fights were rampant. The weaker children were forced to do unspeakable things by and for the other children. They were forced to wash others' clothes and clean the floors and bathrooms and treated like personal servants by the other children. Many were beaten by the group for small infractions like leaving a bed undone or leaving piss on the toilets. Some children were attacked as soon as they walked into the cellblock for being from rival gangs. The guards did not have time to supervise them 24 hours a day. They would walk in to do a count, serve the food, pass out the mail. But, the rest of the time the children were on their own to do as they pleased.

Victor quickly learned that in jail you were either a predator or a prey. There were no grey lines. You either got with the program or were eaten by the wolves. Victor became a wolf. The boxing lessons he had taken as a young teenager helped him survive this place. He was bigger than most kids his age. He was also a very prideful kid. He could not stand ridicule and shame. He had been ashamed of everything as a child and shame was not something he wanted to feel ever again.

In this place he refused to back down from a fight. On the contrary, he looked forward to it. And he won most of them. After a few fights, the other kids began looking to Victor as the leader of the cellblock and his time there was less miserable.

After a year of waiting and waiting, Victor was finally taken to trial. He was represented by a court-appointed attorney because his family was too poor to hire one. The trial was an open and shut case. The state showed evidence that Victor was a gang member, that he was driving the car involved in the drive-by shooting, that the gun was his, and that the victim in this case was his ex-girlfriend's brother.

El Paso was infested with gang activity in those days and Victor knew he was going to get punished severely even though he didn't fully understand what his rights were during the proceedings. His rights were explained at every turn by the judge and the state and his court-appointed attorney, but to Victor they might as well have been talking a foreign language. He didn't understand anything concerning the criminal process. English was his second language. He was a 16-year-old, 9th grade drop-out AND he didn't understand what "due process" and "the 14th Amendment" and those other foreign terms meant! He didn't know what his lawyer meant when he said "law of parties." Victor thought it was a law against parties. As funny as it seems, that was the truth. He didn't understand anything that was going on.

The only other people he could ask questions to were the teenagers of his cellblock and they didn't know shit either.

It did not take long for the jury to come back with a verdict. The judge picked up the verdict from his desk. "All arise!" he said and everyone in the court-room rose to their feet. "The jury has reached a verdict in the case of The State of Texas vs. Victor Adrian Aguirre," he said with a determined voice. He then read the jury's verdict, "We the jury find the defendant, Victor Adrian Aguirre, guilty of murder in the first-degree." Victor could hear the sobs of sadness from his mother and the tears of joy coming from Rigo's family. He felt his knees shaking.

After reading the verdict, the judge read the sentence which the jury had imposed on Victor. He was sentenced to serve 35 years in the Texas Department of Criminal Justice System. He would be a boy among men. With good behavior he would be eligible for release on parole after serving 17 ½ years. That meant that he would be in prison, at the minimum, until he was 34 years old. There was also a possibility that he would never get out. The Texas prison system was known to be a tomb from which many people did not escape.

Victor was devastated. He could not imagine having to spend that many years behind bars. He was only 17 years old for Christ-sakes! He could not understand how he had received so much time. He didn't think he deserved such harsh punishment. He didn't fire the gun! He didn't kill Rigo. He was only a teenager!

He felt dizzy and nauseated. But he could not allow himself to cry or break down. His mother, Guadalupe, had collapsed on the ground sobbing and yelling when the sentence was read. "NO!!! NO!!! NO!!!...Porfavor NO!!!", she pled to the judge, begging for mercy, begging for a miracle for her oldest son. Her sobs sent shivers down the spine.

No miracle would come.

Victor did not want to make things more difficult for her. He wanted to cry. He wanted to scream and yell and plead and ask for another chance. Instead, he sat on his chair stoically staring at the floor. Watching his mom break down was heart wrenching for him. Guadalupe was a strong woman. She did not cry easily. She was the kind of woman who did not ask for help even if she was dying. Her life had been tough. She could take life's punches and her past was a testament to that. But this was too much. She would rather have them rip her heart out than watch her son go to prison for such a long time. To watch her so heart broken, so in pain, was something that Victor would carry in his conscience the rest of his days.

The guards put the shackles and handcuffs on him and walked him down the tunnel back to the jail. It felt like a foggy dream to him. He thought that maybe this was all a nightmare. Tomorrow he would wake up on his bed, sweating and screaming, and realize it was all just a horrible dream. He would get back to his normal life.

This wasn't a dream. He was going to prison and only the gods knew when he would be free again or if fate had other plans for his life.

CHAPTER 7

The House of Detention

"It is said that no one truly knows a nation until one has been inside its jails.
A nation should not be judged by how it treats its highest citizens, but its lowest ones."

-Nelson Mandela

A month after a jury had convicted him and sentenced him, Victor was transferred to the penitentiary. He was woken up in the middle of the night by flashlights in his face and guards screaming for him to get up. The sound of chains echoed throughout the cellblock. All the other children heard the commotion and woke up to see Victor get hauled away. Their looks were that of horror. They had heard about the things that happen to youngsters in prison and they felt fear, and sadness, for him. They also feared the day when it would be their turn to "catch the chain."

Victor was groggy and scared at the same time. He had been waiting for this unexpected moment. He knew he was going to prison but knowing something and actually experiencing it were two different things. For security reasons, the jail authorities do not tell inmates who are going to prison when they will be transferred. They believe that by keeping them in the dark about their transfer, they will be able to prevent orchestrated escape attempts.

Not knowing when he would be transferred was both stressful and a blessing to Victor.

It was stressful because prisons are usually very far away from the cities where most people live and Victor hated not knowing when would be the last day he would be able to see his family consistently. The prison Victor was going to was more than a 12-hour round trip and he was aware that his family would not be able to visit him because they could not afford it. He hated the thought of being so far away, so alone, In an adult and violent environment. What if they killed him in prison? What if they raped him? What if he never saw his daughter again?

But not knowing was also a blessing. Every visit with his mother and his family was treasured. He knew that today might be the day he was taken away and his visits were more urgent. It felt like having a fatal illness, wanting to enjoy every single day because it may be your last.

The handcuffs and shackles were cold on his skin. The guards wrapped him in chains to make sure he could not run. He could barely walk! Every step was a baby step. The chains felt heavy on him. He was taken to a holding area were other guys who were also being transferred were being processed. Now that Victor was convicted, the jail did not have to keep him separated from the adults. He was handcuffed to an older man. There were close to 50 people being transferred that night. Everything seemed like a fog to him. Sadness engulfed him. Fear coursed through his blood.

After everyone was processed and properly chained and shackled, they were led in two-file lines to the "blue bird." The bus was a fortress. Every window was covered with metal. A guard holding a 12-gauge shotgun stood in a cage at the back of the bus. Gates and locks separated the inmates from the guards. Behind the driver another guard faced the inmates with the shotgun on his lap. "If any of you give us any shit, we will blow your fucking head off," that was the warning they received from the bus guards before leaving.

The ride was very uncomfortable. Victor could barely move. He was handcuffed to another inmate and he could not stretch his arms or legs. If anyone wanted to use the bathroom, there was a container at the back where they would have to go – with the other inmate attached to him and everyone else watching. The worse part was that they rode like this for close to 7 hours.

They arrived at the Middleton Unit in Abilene, Texas just as the sun was rising. A group of guards was waiting for them. They screamed for everyone to get off and to "move" their asses. Victor noticed that all of the guards were white. In El Paso he had grown up around Mexicans and other Latinos and the fact that every guard was white was a shock to him. They all seemed to be mad at him and at the world.

One of them grabbed Victor and his partner and slammed them against the bus and told them not to move. He unchained them roughly and pointed for them to follow the other inmates inside.

After everyone was inside, they were lined up and told to strip naked. "Follow my instructions clearly! I will not repeat them and if you do not comply you will be dealt with!", one guard at the front screamed at them. Another guard stood by to conduct the inspection. The commands he gave them were dehumanizing.

"Show me your hands!", one guard barked while the other inspected the hands.

"Open your mouth and show me your tongue!" Everyone opened their mouths and stuck their tongue out.

"Run your fingers through your hair!" Everyone ran their fingers through their hair.

"Lift up your nut-sack!" They all lifted it.

"Now, turn around and show me the bottom of your feet one by one. Right foot! Left foot." Like soldiers everyone followed the instructions.

Then came the worst part. "Okay, now bend over and spread your ass cheeks!" Everyone bent over and spread their ass while the guard looked inside as if he was inspecting the value of a diamond. "If it wasn't so degrading," Victor thought, "this would be funny."

From there they were lined up and forced to shave their head. An inmate barber would cut all their hair off with a few swipes of the hair-clippers and move on to the next person. Everything seemed to run like a well-oiled machine.

Victor loved his hair. It was part of his identity. When he was free, his mom and his friends would tease him because he went the extra mile to keep every single hair strand looking perfect and in place. Now he was being stripped of the only thing he felt was still his. This may have been even more dehumanizing than spreading his ass for the guards.

The prison system wanted it that way. They had a purpose for taking an inmate's identity away. The first thing they took was their name. They gave them a number instead. Victor was no longer Victor. In here he was just #752111. By doing this, the system was punishing them and programming them to feel as if they were no longer part of society. They wanted inmates to feel they were now outcasts who didn't deserve the most basic of things – a name.

Even dogs had names.

Without the guards being aware, they were being dehumanized as well. The system of stripping people of their identities – of turning them into "them" or "the others" - makes it easier to abuse them, and treat them less than human because, hey, they are not like "us." They are not human. Later on, Victor would see this playing out first-hand. He would observe how the guards had no reservation in abusing their authority and doing things to the inmates that normal people wouldn't do.

After a few hours of being processed, finger-printed, searched and photographed, Victor was finally given some sheets and a pillow and escorted to the cellblock he would be housed in.

CHAPTER 8

Running with the Wolves

"We would not be Human if we did not prefer to be the devourers rather than the devoured, but either is a blessing. Should your life be required of you, rest assured that it is required by Life."

-Margaret Atwood, The Year of the Flood

Prison was mind-bogglingly repetitive and monotonous. Every day seemed to be the same as the day before and the day before that. Fights and stabbings and riots were a common occurrence and part of the daily ritual. People were always on edge. A tension always hung thickly in the air. The noise was deafening – bars slamming open or shut, inmates yelling, loud horse playing, dominoes being slammed on metal tables, grunts from workouts, guards talking through the loudspeaker when it was time for "chow" or recreation or commissary. The guards themselves were always screaming over everyone else. They treated the place as their personal property. If you were talking in the hallway, they would say things like, "Stop talking in *my* hallway!!" They always referred to the prison as theirs. "*My* chow hall," "get off of *my* grass," "shut up in *my* yard." Nothing belonged to the inmates, it all belonged to each guard individually.

Victor was very prideful and had a hard time adjusting to prison life. He refused to be treated like an animal or talked to like a child, even though, technically he was a child – he was 17. If a guard gave an order Victor thought was unjust, he would disobey it. Of course, he always paid the consequences. He was constantly being dragged to "the hole" or being punished by the authorities.

Isolation was painful to him. He hated being caged in a cell 24 hours a day without any movement, without any human interaction. But his pride was bigger than his fear of being alone. He hated the guards unnaturally. Some were very kind and professional and treated inmates like human beings, but a lot of them, a huge majority of them, were borderline sadists. They seemed to enjoy abusing their authority and power. Victor made a conscious decision to never allow himself to be ridiculed or disrespected by anyone, especially the guards. He was a walking time bomb. Any little thing would set him off. And we cannot forget the fact that he was still a teenager, with all the raging testosterone itching to let loose.

It wasn't long before prison gang members from El Paso took an interest in Victor. They were always out looking for new recruits.

They wanted to recruit rebellious people. They wanted violence and anger. They wanted people with deep pride who would not back down from anything. These are the attributes they looked for because it was through fear of violence that they held their power and controlled people inside the prison walls and beyond. People had to be scared of them if they wanted to wield their power and the only way people would be scared of them is if they had violent members who would stop at nothing to reach whatever objective the gang had. Victor was a perfect candidate for a prison gang.

In a few months of prison life, he had already made a statement to the guards and to the inmates that he was not going to take any shit. It had cost him dearly, of course. He had been in isolation for most of his time so far. But he felt pride when a prison gang began recruiting him. He was young, but they obviously didn't see him as a kid. He took that as an honor.

He began hanging around with the gang almost 24 hours a day. He began learning their rules and their ideas. They seemed to have the entire prison under their control. They seemed to be very organized and powerful. Even the guards seemed to fear them.

He became what they called a "prospecto", a prospect. As a prospect, Victor had to do a lot of the dirty work for the gang. If someone needed a beating, the prospects took care of it. If drugs needed to be transported to another cellblock, prospects transported them. If extortion fees had to be collected, they collected them. Victor didn't like being a prospect. He felt it was beneath him. He didn't like taking orders and being treated like a personal servant for members of the gang. But this was the process that must be followed if Victor wanted to become a "made" member of the gang and he followed the rules as best he could.

After a year of being a prospect, Victor was given the opportunity to become a member. The only problem was that in these gangs you didn't just go through an "initiation" where you had to fight a few members. That was not good enough. Here, with these gangs, things were more serious. It was known as "blood in, blood out." This meant that you had to shed someone's blood to get in and shed your own if you wanted out. There was no getting out of these gangs. If you wanted to quit, you would be a target to get killed. This was explained to Victor numerous times during his "prospecto" phase. He really didn't care. He was beginning to feel and think that he would never see freedom again. He felt this was his life and being part of the gang was something he wanted to do for as long as he was here. This would become the family he was always chasing. He had no plans of ever quitting the gang.

To become a member Victor was given a "camello" (hit) to do. If he completed this hit successfully, he would earn the membership he had worked to earn for the past year.

The hit was ordered against a guy on the unit who was a former member of the gang. He thought nobody knew about him. He walked around the prison without a care in the world knowing that the other inmates did not recognize him. He knew that if the gang found out about him, they would send someone to stab and try to kill him. Those were the rules.

He had been transferred to this unit years ago and no one had found him out. He had been on edge the first few years because he knew he was on their hit list. Just like every other member of the gang, before he joined, it was explained to him that he could never quit, or else. He knew it. And he had quit. But the years had passed and no one had noticed or recognized him.

Until now.

Someone had whispered to the gang that a former member of theirs was on this unit under cover and that he had been right under their noses for years. The gang investigated the situation.

They held secret meetings in the yard to discuss what was happening and, sure enough, after weeks of investigation this guy turned out to be a former member of theirs who had called it quits. Their blood in, blood out rule required that he be stabbed and eliminated. A vote was taken and the decision was unanimous – kill him. They were furious because this guy had been right in front of them and embarrassed them with other gangs. They looked like a bunch of fools and now he must pay dearly.

Victor was given the order for the hit. This was his last test as a prospect. He had not been allowed to participate in the official gang meetings concerning this situation. He did not get to vote. He was just a prospect. But he was chosen to carry out the hit. To make sure the hit was done correctly, Tommy, a ranking member of the gang, would accompany Victor and they both would make sure the debt against the gang was paid.

Victor was given a "shank," a hand-made knife used in prison stabbings. Tommy had his own shank as well. They waited in the prison cafeteria for the ex-member to show up. Victor was nervous. He knew that stabbing someone was serious business. If caught, he would end up in solitary confinement indefinitely and would get more years added to his 35-year sentence. He would never be able to hug his daughter or his family again during visits. He would be in a cell by himself for the rest of his time. If prison authorities proved you were a gang member, they had the authority to put you in isolation forever if they wanted to. In isolation, all privileges (like contact visits, and recreation, and education), were terminated. Victor needed to do this without being caught.

He was also nervous because the gang expected this hit to be used as an example to other members who thought about quitting the gang. It needed to be vicious and savage. It would show everyone that this gang did not play when it felt disrespected or when its rules were broken.

His stomach was full of nervous butterflies. He saw and felt his body shaking from fear. Tommy, who had a life sentence, was sitting next to him smiling and telling him to calm down. Tommy had nothing to lose. He was never going home. Stabbing someone was like eating ice cream at the park for him.

When the ex-member walked into the cafeteria, Victor and Tommy prepared to attack. They waited until the perfect moment, when they could lose themselves in the crowd, and then they would pounce. The ex-member did not know it was coming. They wiggled around people to get close to him.

He was not aware they were here for him. He kept laughing and talking to the guy next to him unaware that they were right behind him waiting for the perfect time.

When Tommy saw the guard on duty turn around away from them, he jumped and started the stabbing. Victor was right behind. They stabbed him in a frenzy. Tommy looked like a lion on a hyena. He was possessed. Victor almost stabbed Tommy in the confusion of it all. The ex-member attempted to run. Victor stabbed him quickly on his ribs. Once, twice, three times.

Everything was a blur. Sound did not exist for what seemed like forever.

Victor could hear guards yelling and screaming for everyone, "Get on the floor! Get on the floor!"

Tommy handed his shank to Victor. "Pierdelos," lose them, he instructed. Victor ducked and hid amongst the crowd of inmates who were trying to get on the floor. Victor saw some buckets full of waste-food and threw both shanks in one of them. He then threw himself on the floor and lay as still as a log, making sure not to draw any attention to himself. He slowly wiped some blood from his hands.

The ex-member was carted off the cafeteria and rushed to the prison hospital. He was covered in blood and seemed to be unconscious. They later found out he survived the attack, but just barely.

Tommy had blood on him and was caught for the stabbing. He was dragged to the hole. Victor made it past the guard's inspection and investigation and suffered no consequences for the incident. The entire prison was placed on a 30-day lock-down to investigate further and ensure nothing else was going to happen. Soon after, Victor became one the youngest official member of the gang.

He was conflicted.

He had become a made member. But, at what cost? He had almost killed someone. He had brutally stabbed another person. In front of his new "brothers" he was the personification of someone who didn't give a damn. He acted as if the stabbing had taken no toll on his emotions. But it had. This was not who he was. He remembered the words his mother had told him years ago: "Why are you trying to be someone you are not?"

Being a member of the gang came with many privileges. Victor would get a cut of all drug sales and extortions made in prison, and out in the streets, by the gang. Every member had to be taken care of evenly. It also brought him protection from other gangs or inmates. No one wanted to mess with a made gang member because he knew the gang would retaliate in full force if one of its members had been "disrespected." And, as always, Victor felt like he had found his family once again. In a place so far away from home, it felt good to belong to a group of people you felt were like brothers to you.

But, just like all things in this world, everything come with a price.

CHAPTER 9

The Isolation Transformation

"The eternal quest of the individual human being is to shatter his loneliness."

-Norman Cousins

After a few years of being in the prison gang, Victor was becoming exhausted with his membership. He was getting older and he began to realize that one day, a few years down the road, he would be eligible for release on parole. If he kept doing all the stupid things he was doing now that opportunity would go down the drain.

He was also having conflicting emotions about some of the gang's rules. By nature, prison gangs are racist organizations made up of members from one race or the other. Most prison gangs do not allow people of a different race than theirs to join their ranks. There are a few exceptions, but it is the exception, not the rule.

Vicor's gang rules prohibited him from hanging around with black inmates. Blacks were seen as an enemy and the gang demanded that its members keep their distance from them. They were not to eat with them, exercise with them, or do anything that appeared to be friendly towards them.

Victor's thinking had evolved and matured. He had met black guys who he got along with just fine and didn't see a problem in building friendships with them or any other race. It wasn't just black people the gang prohibited building relationships with. All gang members ate together, hung around the yard together, went to the dayroom to watch movies together. Hanging around or building strong relationships with other inmates who were not part of the gang, whatever their race, was frowned upon.

There were times when Victor did not want to fight or battle with the people the gang wanted to fight or battle with. Victor was not a violent person – as ironic as that sounds. He wanted what every other normal person yearned for – peace and tranquillity. He did not want to fight or stab or hurt. He wanted to live and let live. He hated hurting people. From the outside you would never be able to tell that this is how he felt. But he did. He hated a lot of the things he did as a gang member.

More than anything, Victor was starting to become more aware that his daughter Sylvia was growing up without him and he began to feel a big responsibility towards her. She was growing fast. He had been able to visit with her a couple of times over the years and holding her in his arms was one of the best feelings in the world for him.

He specifically remembered the first time he was able to have a contact visit with her. Sylvia was six years old at the time and when she saw him walk into the visiting room she ran and jumped into his arms. Her laugh and giggles of glee brought tears to his eyes. Throughout the visit Sylvia clung to him with her arms around his shoulders and would not let go. She told him everything about her little life, about her tiny friends and about how she wished he was home to play with her. That visit stuck with him and stirred something inside him. It meant more to him now that he was older and more mature. He had begun to feel a desire to be someone Sylvia could be proud of.

A few months after turning 24 years old, his gang membership cost him dearly. Another gang hit in the recreation yard resulted in five members of the gang being taken away to solitary confinement. Victor was included. Someone had been brutally beaten and was in the hospital fighting for his life. A helicopter had to be called to transport the guy to emergency care.

Victor's past prison disciplinary file was huge and prison authorities had begun keeping an eye on him as a possible leader of the gang. Since his gang had been the one responsible for the hit, prison officials felt Victor had been involved in the planning of the attack and took him to the hole along with 4 other members of the gang.

As devastating as this news was for Victor, the hole would become the turning point in his life. Being locked in a small cage 24 hours a day was a horrible existence. It was like living inside your own head. No human contact. All you had was your thoughts. Some people literally lost their minds in that environment. The only time you left the cell was to the shower room and it was always with your hands cuffed behind your back and a baton-carrying guard on each side of you.

This extreme isolation turned out to be the blessing Victor needed to make a change from within. Having nothing else to do, he began reading voraciously. Sometimes he would finish a book in one day. He fell passionately in love with books. He became lost in them. In their pages he found an escape from the harsh reality he was living in. At first, he would read only novels, especially from Stephen King and Dean Koonts. But then he began reading self-help books: philosophy, psychology, anything educational. He loved the written word. Not being able to have any human contact, Victor found that reading books was like having a conversation with the authors or the characters in them. Books became his salvation. They completely transformed his thinking and his lifestyle.

He also began to write in a journal/diary. At first it seemed pointless to him. "What will I write about! It is the same thing every day in this place!" he thought to himself. However, as each day passed by, he noticed his writing touched on different subjects that were interesting to him. He made keen observations about his environment. He saw humor and sadness and strength being displayed every day. But his writing also started touching on something very sensitive: his past. Victor had never dealt with or thought about his past before. Maybe he had done it subconsciously. However, with his writing, he was beginning to probe this difficult subject head on. He wrote about it, analyzed it, felt the emotions brought up with it – the anger, the shame, the guilt, the pain. It was very difficult! But it was necessary and therapeutic for him. Without knowing it, he was doing exactly what needed to be done for healing to begin – acceptance and letting go.

Most importantly, Victor began to take college courses through correspondence. He had finished his high school diploma not long after entering prison, but this was the first time he had made a decision to study hard and get a degree. He took paralegal courses from a well-known law school and became a certified prison lawyer, known as a "prison writ-writer." From his little cage, he began helping other inmates appeal their convictions or

fight for their rights in prison. He became a full-time prison activist.

Other inmates would look for his counsel when it came to any legal matters. In prison, legal matters were not in short supply. He spent hours writing about prison issues, about poverty, about gangs, to his fellow inmates. His writing was not an official newsletter, but other inmates began to expect his writing every week because he always had interesting information or commentaries about issues which pertained to them. He loved doing the research and the writing. It kept him busy and feeling useful.

For three and a half years this was his life in isolation. In that hellish place, he felt freer than he had ever felt in his life. He felt useful, fulfilled, balanced. He looked forward to the next moment. The guards would sometimes tease him because they would pass by his cell and he would be sitting on the floor, surrounded by legal books and documents, taking notes like a madman.

After three and a half years of living in complete solitude, a committee of prison officials known as the State Classification Committee, interviewed Victor for possible release from the hole back to the general population of the prison. Victor was giddy with excitement. He missed playing basketball and handball with

other inmates. He missed having contact visits with his daughter and family. He missed hanging out in the yard and lifting weights. He missed socializing, period!

Due to his good behavior in the hole, and because he was taking college correspondence courses, the State Classification Committee voted on his behalf. He would be released back to the regular population immediately. They gave him a strong warning about gang activity. They promised to keep him in the hole forever if he committed another gang act.

However, his mind had totally been transformed in isolation. Reading and writing had opened his eyes to a new way of seeing things, a new way of seeing himself and others. He no longer felt shame. He was at peace with himself and his past. Participating in gang activity was nowhere in his radar.

CHAPTER 10

A CHANGE IS GONNA COME

"There have been times that I thought I couldn't last for long
But now I think I'm able to carry on
It's been a long, a long time coming
But I know a change is gonna come, oh yes it will."
- Sam Cooke

Back in the regular prison population Victor began to thrive even more than in isolation. Leaders and members from his own gang began to respect the change they were seeing in him and left him out of gang activities. For the next nine years he became very active in prison reform and was in the middle of any and all activities he saw as transforming the prison environment.

He filed lawsuits and grievances to help make needed changes to the "system." He participated in, or organized, hunger-strikes or work-strikes if he felt the cause was just. He helped other inmates, who had no money for attorneys, with their appeals or by explaining the criminal system process in ways they could understand. The better informed they were, he believed, the better decisions they would be able to make concerning their cases. He helped overturn two wrongful convictions and this turned him into a prison legend in the legal field. In Prison, "writ writers" or prison lawyers, most of the time, are known as phonies who pretend to know the law just to make a dollar from the ignorance of other inmates. This belief is true most of the time. By helping to overturn two convictions and getting numerous results with other documents he filed, Victor had gained credibility and credibility in prison can take you a long way.

One of Victor's proudest moments was when he became a member of a powerful organization called Texas CURE (Citizens United for the Rehabilitation of Errants). This organization was made up of free-world citizens who believed the prison system, in its current form, was broken, dysfunctional and harmed society more than it benefits it. Through, and with, this organization, he fought for better treatment of inmates, their families, and victim's families.

Of course, prison officials did not like this new version of Victor. They didn't like him running around trying to "fix" things. He was a nuisance to them. He didn't care. He had found his voice. He had found what he was passionate about (justice) and he gave everything of himself for this passion. Before, Victor had given everything of himself for the gangs he was part of. Now he refocused his energies to peace and justice and was content and fulfilled.

Years later, after 21 ½ years in prison, Victor was getting ready to see the parole board – a group of people who would decide whether or not to release Victor from prison – for the third time. He had been denied release two times before. He had spent over half his life in prison – half of his teens, all of his 20's and half of his 30's. He was totally different than the child he had been back then when he first started his prison stint. He had matured not only in age but in his mentality. As he looked back to all the decisions he had made, he felt ashamed of many of them. He had caused a lot of pain to his family, to others and to himself. But he had also come to accept the fact that we must all travel the road we have been assigned to travel. This whole experience, from childhood to now, was *his* journey.

It had been difficult, but very worth it. He had lost so much…and gained even more. He was finally at peace with himself and nothing could ever take that from him.

The interview with the parole commissioner (the lead voter of the parole board) was different this time around. Texas CURE had used social media to talk about Victor's case. They felt, just as Victor felt, that a 35-year sentence was a harsh sentence for his role in the crime. Because he was a 16-year-old juvenile at the time of the crime, many people believed Victor deserved another chance at freedom, especially because he had not fired any of the shots that killed Rigo.

His sister Mireya had remained his most loyal supporter and helped spearhead the movement asking for his release. Many people from around the world signed a petition and sent letters to the parole board on his behalf. The director of Texas Cure, Michael Jewell, met personally with one of the board members to discuss Victor's case.

The most important thing Victor had going for him was the fact that the victim's family, his daughter's family, had witnessed his transformation from afar and were in support of his release as well. They called the board and sent letters to them. They requested that he be released this time around.

At the interview, the parole commissioner asked him questions about the crime. He asked questions about his disciplinary record and about his educational achievements. It was stressful for Victor because he knew this interview had the power to give him his freedom – something he had yearned for so many years. In the past, there had been days when Victor would feel helpless and think he would never see the free world again. At one point, he even contemplated suicide. He would rather die than spend his whole life in prison.

The parole commissioner had a poker face. Victor could not read it. He could not tell which way the commissioner was leaning. The conversation went on for about an hour. The commissioner told Victor he had to give the case more thought. He had to talk it over with the rest of the board and then they would make a final decision and notify him of it.

Victor left the parole interview optimistic but cautious. He knew he had a lot of support from outside. But he also knew the parole board was an independent entity and made their own decision without regard to public opinion. The next few days were the most stressful days of his life to that point. He could not sleep. He waited and waited to get notified.

There were different ways for the board to notify him of their decision. They could send it through the mail to him. They could call him in again and tell him, or they would make it public on the prison computer system so his family members could tell him. Every time the mail was passed Victor would get nervous. When no mail arrived with his name, he had conflicting emotions. He felt good because no answer was a good answer. But he also wanted the answer now! Not tomorrow or the day after.

Five days after his interview the answer arrived. Victor was called to the prison office and told that his sister Mireya needed to talk to him urgently. Victor ran back to the cellblock and jumped on the phone immediately. He knew Mireya had an answer for him. The board must have put the answer on the computer system and Mireya knew what it was.

When she answered, her voice was cracking and laughing at the same time. "I have some good news for you Vic............YOU ARE COMING HOME!!! YOU ARE FINALLY COMING HOME!!"

Her tears of joy tugged his heart strings and tears bubbled up in his eyes. He could not believe it. After 21 ½ years he was finally going home. He was speechless. All he could do was giggle into the phone. Mireya told him to hurry up and call his daughter because she wanted to talk to him and share the good news with him as well.

When Sylvia answered it was the same thing as Mireya. She was yelling into the phone in celebration. She had waited for this day, literally, her whole life! She was three months old when Victor had been taken away. In a few months she would turn 22. All her life was spent waiting for her father to return and now it was happening. It was an incredible feeling for both of them. Victor remembered the first time he had hugged her from behind bars when she was 6 years old. Now she had become a beautiful woman, even though, in his memory, she would always remain the little girl from that day long ago.

CHAPTER 11

Redemption

"Was it you or I who stumbled first? It does not matter. The one of us who finds
the strength to get up first, must help the other."

-Vera Nazarian

When Victor finally stepped out of the prison gates the world he saw was like another planet. Everything was different. Cars were different. The technology available was like from another dimension. He felt overpowering emotions of happiness and fulfillment. He wanted to run through the streets and scream out his happiness. It was like he had been raised from the dead. It was exhilarating. He no longer had to ask permission to use the bathroom, to walk somewhere. He would no longer be told when to work, when to eat, when to sleep. He was free to walk in the rain, to breathe deeply and smell the wet-dirt under his feet. He could finally own a dog. It had been years since he had last seen or petted one. He loved all animals, but especially dogs.

I know how he felt because Victor is me. This is a true story. My story. I was released from prison after serving 21 ½ years of a 35-year sentence. I began to write this short story of my life as therapy. It felt good to let some things go through the pen and onto paper. Later on, I kept writing because I felt it was important to share my story.

I remember one particular incident which convinced me my story must be told. It was not long after I was released. I was scheduled to meet with Beatriz Flores. She was a psychologist working with children in one of the poorest areas of Puerto Vallarta known as "el basurero" – the dump. In this community, she was in charge of many things. She helped with the children's education, took them to the hospital when needed, and helped resolve many of the problems that arise in extremely poor communities like the one she was working in.

I had met her the week before while I was doing volunteer construction work in this "colonia" (neighborhood). We had a chance encounter and began to talk. I explained that I had just arrived to Puerto Vallarta and that I needed to find a job. She asked me about my educational background and when I told her, she asked me to meet with her in her office in a few days to help me make a resume. She was sure I would find a job immediately. That night, Glenn, a Christian guy I had met and was hanging around with, told me to not say anything about my prison stay to Beatriz.

"If you tell her you've been in prison, there is a high probability that she will judge you and decide not to help you at all. It's better if you just stay quiet about your past. With her and with everybody," he said.

I listened without showing how bothered I was at what he said. This had upset me deeply. I stayed up all night thinking about what Glenn had told me. For the first time in a long time I felt shame creeping back into my mind.

"Should I tell people about my past? Or should I keep quiet and lie about it, pretend to be someone I'm not?" The thoughts kept running wild in my head. Maybe he was right. Maybe people would judge me by my past.

I wrestled with a decision for a few days. But, after being honest with myself, I knew I would never hide from my past. I was not ashamed of it. I really wasn't. I didn't see it as a representation of who I was now. I actually saw my past as a loyal friend who had wanted to mold me and shape me into a good human being. The past had helped me find peace within myself, how could I ignore it and throw it by the wayside like a useless rag?

The meeting with Beatriz went better than expected. Being a psychologist, she was a very good listener and made me feel comfortable when I told her my story. At one point she had tears in her eyes. I was glad I had chosen to tell my story and tell it proudly.

I also wanted to share my story through this book because I know there are a lot of people in the world who have their own stories of struggle and survival. Most of us have a story to tell. I have met people who I would have never imagined had a past like they have had. I have heard stories of sexual abuse and rapes, of dysfunctional family backgrounds, of deaths, of unspeakable pain and sorrow. There are many people who have gone through unimaginable situations.

But, almost always, the people who have moved on to happy and fulfilling lives, speak about those situations as learning experiences or as situations which made them stronger and helped them turn into more complete human beings.

As much as we hate it, suffering seems to have a purpose for those who are willing to see their suffering from that perspective. And when I say suffering, I mean suffering caused by others towards us or suffering created from our own negative actions and decisions.

The benefits of suffering are many. Because of our suffering, we develop our capacity for empathy. It is easier to empathize with someone's situation when you yourself have been through something similar or have felt the powerlessness and despair that come from suffering. We know how it feels because we have felt the same: we have been in somebody else's shoes

Suffering also breeds humility. "When everything is going our way, it's easy to become so caught up in our own busy world that we may overlook or diminish the challenges faced by those who are doing it tough. Some people become arrogant and judgmental, perhaps believing they are somehow immune to the problems that, in time, we all must face. When we suffer, we know the truth. There is no place to be a big deal. And with humility, we develop gratitude for things we may have overlooked: the kindness of friends and strangers. The happiness to be found in everyday things."

There is no doubt suffering makes us stronger. However, we have to "choose" to see it that way. "Everything can be taken from a man but one thing: the last of the human freedoms—to choose one's attitude in any given set of circumstances, to choose one's own way," says Viktor Frankl in my favorite book, Man's Search for Meaning.

There are only two choices we can make when we suffer. Either we choose to use it for growth and learning, or we let our circumstances defeat us and eat us slowly from within. When I was in prison, I met people on both sides of the spectrum. There were guys who had only months to be released but complained about everything and continued to see themselves as victims. They blamed everyone else for their situations: their parents, their spouse, society. Some of them had legit grievances against people or institutions who had hurt them. But they had not chosen to rise above it, to make peace with that suffering and use it as a springboard for growth. This kept them miserable and unhappy. They found no meaning for their lives.

On the other hand, there were guys who were serving life sentences and were never going to see the streets again but had found meaning in their suffering. They had very productive lives. They were active in the church community or became paralegals. They organized recreation activities. They found a way to give meaning to their lives despite their circumstances. They helped and volunteered their time to others when possible. They found a meaning for their lives. "Those who have a 'why' to live, can bear with almost any 'how'," Viktor Frankl writes.

Again, most of us have our own histories. We have had our share of individual struggles and will face struggles in the future. I write this book for you. I ask you to choose to rise above it, to use your suffering for growth and betterment, to find your "why" so you can bear any "how."

Even if you are in a situation which is unbearable right now this very moment, change your attitude towards it. Do not let your circumstances rob you of "the last of the human freedoms," the freedom to choose your attitude. I was in solitary confinement, in a 7 x 9 cell which looked like something from the medieval days, when I chose to change my attitude towards life. My life to that point had been one big catastrophe. Viktor Frankl was in a Nazi concentration camp when he made *his* choice. No matter where you find yourself now, whether it is a physical or metaphorical prison, you have the ability to choose. Take it and make it count for something.

I truly believe we all have a personal journey to travel. There is a purpose to every single one of our lives. Sometimes things happen to us that we just can't understand. Death, poverty, hunger, sickness, destruction, tragedies - they are all part of the human experience. Each one of us goes through his or her own ordeals and triumphs. We cannot escape some of the things that will happen to us. They are inevitable at times. We won't understand it and we won't be able to see logic or reason behind it. Shit happens, as crude as that may sound. But there is always hope.

If you are alive, there is always time to write a new page, to have a new start, to begin a new story. That time is called NOW. Your past does not have to define who you are NOW. Quit holding onto the baggage of the past. Embrace it. Deal with it. Work with it. It is your friend. Let it guide you and help you become the best version of yourself.

EPILOGUE

And what ever happened to this beautiful lady Beatriz (Bety) who helped me with my resume and who listened so lovingly to my crazy story? We became very good friends. We started working on projects together. We fell in love. A year after we met, we were married in a beautiful beach ceremony. My best friend, Pastor Frank Natera, whom I met in a juvenile detention center and who served 21 years in prison along with me, presided over the wedding.

Bety and I always laugh because we make the oddest of couples. She was raised in a very loving middle-class family. She graduated with a Master's Degree in Psychology. In San Francisco, California, she helped ex-convicts and homeless people in various ways through a shelter she helped run. Our paths were on opposite sides and they merged at the perfect moment. For some reason, we make a great team. She is the intellect and I am the muscle. Okay, the flabby muscle.

In early 2017 I found a job as an English teacher at a school called the Volcanes Kids Education Project. This school is located in one of the poorest "colonias" of Puerto Vallarta, Jalisco, Mexico and serves the disadvantaged children in the area. I love working there. The majority of these kids come from backgrounds of extreme poverty like the ones I grew up in. Some of our students are living in situations that shock the conscience and crush the soul.

I do not think it is a coincidence that I am there. Education was what totally transformed *my* life. It is because of education that I was able to follow a new road and be where I am today. It is only logical that God would put me in a place like this, a place where I can use education to change children's lives.

I originally found out about this school through my wife (she was my friend back then). Apart from being a psychologist, she is also the Vice President of an organization called The Solidarity Foundation. Through this foundation, she was implementing a savings program at the school to teach kids the value of saving. I went along to help her. When we arrived, I was astonished to see a bunch of students, mainly 11 to 14-year olds, sweeping, mopping and watering the plants and trees. I later found out that the students were in charge of cleaning the entire school.

I began volunteering at the project. Soon after, one of the English teachers was dismissed and I was asked to help with the English classes, "for a few weeks until we find a teacher," the director told me. I was glad to do it. The only problem was that I had never taught before. I was a paralegal and knew nothing about teaching. But I went in head first and did the best I could. It was a challenge. What made it easier is that I love kids. They have no agendas, they tell you things as they perceive them, and that's that. I am the oldest of 6 siblings and, growing up with so many kids around, I can relate to them.

After a few weeks, the director called me into her office and asked me if I wanted to be the full time English teacher. I was a little scared. However, I could not refuse this opportunity. I was actually humbled by the request. The director knew my story. Before I began volunteering at the project, I had been interviewed by her and had told her my story. She did not judge me and allowed me to volunteer. Now she was asking me to be the teacher.

"I understand you have no teaching experience, Victor. However, I have been a teacher for a long time. Teaching is about attitude, about caring. I am offering you the job because you have what it takes. The students gravitate towards you and you have made a connection with them. You have the attitude we are looking for. If you accept, I will hire you on the condition you take a teaching course. We will get you a scholarship for the courses."

I was shocked. I accepted immediately. This was my dream job. I valued education because I knew from personal experience what it could do to transform lives: education had changed *my* life. I began as the full-time 5th and 6th grade English teacher the next day. Immediately thereafter I enrolled in an English teaching program and became a certified English Teacher.

The surprise of a lifetime came a year and a half later. The director and her husband (both were the founders of the school) invited my wife and I to dinner. I was a bit worried and thought that maybe I was going to get bad news from them. I kept going over the past few days trying to remember anything I may have done wrong. I could think of nothing that would warrant being fired.

To my surprise, it was the complete opposite.

"Victor, we have been very impressed with your work at the school. You have done a very good job with your classes and we are impressed with the results," Mr. Art Fumerton told me as he shook my hand shortly after my wife and I approached the table.

"I have been thinking of retiring for some time and have been looking for someone to take my place at the school. Someone with the same vision as we have for our programs," Mrs. Mayra, the director, added. "We would like to offer you the job of Director of the Volcanes Kids Education Program."

What!? The director? Of an entire school? I could not believe it. To say I was astonished is an understatement. Just a few years earlier I had been in prison. Heck, only a year and six months had passed since I became a teacher. Now they were asking me to run an entire school. It was crazy! I couldn't speak. I was in shock. The flurry of emotions wanted to burst through my eyes.

After gaining my composure, I told them I would be happy to accept the job offer. And that is where I am working now - as the Director of the Volcanes Kids Education Program.

In 2018 I was also able to start a free soccer league to allow kids in the poorest neighborhoods of Puerto Vallarta to play soccer. Most of these kids, especially the ones living in the dump area, cannot afford to play in regular leagues. They cannot afford to pay the registration fees, uniform fees, etcetera. With the help of many people in Puerto Vallarta, the league has grown to 16 teams.

In an ironic twist, two police officers from the Puerto Vallarta Police force are working with me coaching some of our teams. One of them is a Comandante (Commander) in the police force. Our main sponsor and supporter, Tom Mueller, is a retired United

States Army Lieutenant. Talk about an unlikely partnership – the ex-convict/gang member working with police and military officers.

It has been amazing to witness how, all along, from childhood until now, my life has been on the road to redemption.

INVICTUS

Out of the night that covers me,
Black as the pit from pole to pole,
I thank whatever gods may be
For my unconquerable soul.

In the fell clutch of circumstance
I have not winced nor cried aloud.
Under the bludgeonings of chance
My head is bloody, but unbowed.

Beyond this place of wrath and tears
Looms but the horror of the shade,
And yet the menace of the years
Finds and shall find me unafraid.

It matters not how strait the gate,
How charged with punishments the scroll,
I am the master of my fate:
I am the captain of my soul.

-

- **William Ernest Henley (1849-1903)**

About the Author

Victor Adrian Aguirre Roman is the Director of the Volcanes Kids Education Project and President of the non-profit Educacion y Deportes Para Una Vida Mejor in Puerto Vallarta, Jalisco, Mexico. He spent 21 ½ years in the Texas Department of Criminal Justice Department for a crime committed when he was 16 years old. His road to redemption continues.

For more information about the Volcanes Kids Education Program visit their website at www.volcanesproject.com

Last of the Human Freedoms

Last of the Human Freedoms

Last of the Human Freedoms

Made in the USA
San Bernardino, CA
29 May 2019